MW01594887

HEALING A *mother's* GRIEVING HEART

31-DAY DEVOTIONAL

BY REBECCA DEMATTIA, LCSW-C

A wholly owned subsidiary of TBN

Healing A Mother's Grieving Heart
Trilogy Christian Publishers
A Wholly Owned Subsidiary of Trinity Broadcasting Network
2442 Michelle Drive
Tustin, CA 92780

Copyright © 2022 by Rebecca DeMattia

Scripture quotations marked (NIV) are taken from the Holy Bible, New International Version®, NIV®. Copyright © 1973, 1978, 1984, 2011 by Biblica, Inc.TM Used by permission of Zondervan. All rights reserved worldwide. www.zondervan.com. The "NIV" and "New International Version" are trademarks registered in the United States Patent and Trademark Office by Biblica, Inc.TM

Scripture quotations marked (NLT) are from the New Living Translation Bible. Copyright© Used by permission of NavPress. All rights reserved. Represented by Tyndale House Publishers, a Division of Tyndale House Ministries.

For information, address Trilogy Christian Publishing
Rights Department, 2442 Michelle Drive, Tustin, CA 92780.
Trilogy Christian Publishing/ TBN and colophon are trademarks of Trinity Broadcasting Network.
For information about special discounts for bulk purchases, please contact Trilogy Christian Publishing.
Manufactured in the United States of America
Trilogy Disclaimer: The views and content expressed in this book are those of the author and may not necessarily reflect the views and doctrine of Trilogy Christian Publishing or the Trinity Broadcasting Network.
10 9 8 7 6 5 4 3 2 1
Library of Congress Cataloging-in-Publication Data is available.
ISBN: 979-8-88738-081-0
ISBN: 979-8-88738-082-7

Introduction

If you are reading this book, that means you are a grieving mother, and first, let me say I am sorry. There are no words that begin to express the sorrow a mother's heart feels when she is in the sea of grief. No matter your child's age, whether in your womb or outside your house, your heart grieves the same. I want you to remember that no matter how many children you are grieving, no matter the circumstances around their death and no matter the details, YOU ARE ALLOWED TO GRIEVE. Perhaps your loss was a pregnancy that only showed positive for twenty-four hours on an at-home test, or your child was a grown adult with children of their own living far away. Maybe you weren't close to your child; you were estranged or separated or something else. No matter the circumstances, you are allowed to be in a season of grief. Grief and loss are not a competition or a comparison game about whose loss is more complex or deserving of recognition. All deaths and losses are valid, necessary to recognize, and, more importantly, allowed to be processed and honored.

If you have read this far, I am grateful. This book comes from a place of my own grief journey. I am currently the mother of two beautiful girls; however, I have five angel babies. My journey to motherhood was marked with pain, loss, frustration, confusion, anger, hopelessness, grief, and sadness. Before I gave birth to my first daughter, I experienced two early miscarriages at six weeks: then a traumatic miscarriage at sixteen weeks, Gracie. Gracie was a viable, healthy pregnancy until it wasn't. Everything was going well until our sixteen-week appointment, and the doctor didn't hear a heartbeat. The loss of Gracie was traumatic, and I endured labor and an emergency d&c at our local hospital. My heart was changed that day.

I sank into a deep and unforgiving depression and contemplated taking my own life. It was a dark time in my life, and if it weren't for my faith in God and the story of Hannah and Samuel from the Bible, I know I wouldn't be here. I had another miscarriage after Gracie, again at six weeks, then my life shifted, and I went through an ugly divorce. The loss of my babies didn't cause the divorce, but it surely didn't help a troubled marriage survive. Fast forward a few years, and I got remarried to the man of my dreams. After one year of marriage, we decided that we would begin to try and have a child, and I miscarriage again but this time after only a few days of showing positive. The doctors called this a chemical pregnancy, but my heart was still shattered. Due to all my losses previously, I was referred to fertility treatments. I was hopeful, excited, and nervous.

Being a mother was something I had always wanted. It was a part of my five-year/ten-year life goals. You know the ones they make you complete when you are younger… where do I see myself in five years? I had dreams, aspirations, goals! And being a mother was close to the top. My husband was super supportive and way more optimistic than I was. So, fertility treatment began, all the blood-work, tests, and scans looked great. We were candidates for IUI treatments, and the doctor and nurses were confident we would come through this with a baby. I endured three failed IUI treatments, and I was crushed. My poor husband wasn't around for Gracie's death and previous miscarriages, so he didn't completely understand my deep, endless sorrow. The doctors didn't have a good reason why the IUI treatments didn't "take," but were working on our next plan. I wasn't thrilled about undergoing more treatments, but we had one more IUI treatment left to finish before looking into IVF. My husband and I discussed it, and I couldn't emotionally handle another failed attempt, so we took a month off from all treatments and went on a vacation. Miraculously, we became pregnant on our own. Let me tell you that I was paranoid most of that pregnancy. The doctors were excited that we had a natural pregnancy, and one of the perks of being in infertility treatments was regular screenings and sonograms. I had the joy of watching my peanut grow from week to week. And although it was amazing to be monitored so closely, I couldn't help that I was in a constant state of dread and pessimism; I thought for sure I would lose this baby too. Once I made it to eighteen weeks, I felt slightly better but still paranoid of every cramp, every change in discharge, every slight pain or twinge. I am blessed to say that I made it through that pregnancy, full-term, and my beautiful Sofia was born healthy and happy.

Given my journey this far, I was happy and content with being a mom to one living, breathing baby and felt selfish and ungrateful even to think or pray for another. However, my husband knew that we were destined to be parents to at least two children. We were on vacation with our family when we conceived, by accident, our second daughter. Like all the other pregnancies, I was paranoid, uncertain, and simply scared of losing this baby. That pregnancy was eventless, and I had my Zoe full-term and healthy! I thought that two babies were my limit, and again I was perfectly content with two babies. However, I became pregnant once again, unexpectedly, but this pregnancy ended in another traumatic miscarriage at nine weeks, but this time I was at home with my mom and husband. The loss of this baby flooded my senses with grief all over again. All the sadness, loss, anger, confusion instantly came back to me. I had wrestled with this last pregnancy, not entirely content with having another baby, and the timing was less than ideal. Then when I lost it, I felt overwhelmingly guilty for almost feeling as though I wished this baby away. My head knew that this wasn't the truth; no one has that much control. But the guilt was real, just as it was with the other four miscarriages, just as it was when I lost Gracie; just as it is now as I write these words to you. But then I remember the words…BUT GOD…

God, in His infinite wisdom and plan, is there to comfort, heal, to guide. I may not even know His plan or reasoning on why I endured so many angel babies, but I do know that through this journey, I have been able to hold the hands of other mothers and cry and comfort them. Without our big God and His big plan, we cannot survive the fire of trial, trauma, and pain. God gives us the Holy Spirit to speak to us in times of distress, grief, and sadness, and my hope in the pages of this devotional is to allow God to heal your heart, soften your defenses and bring down your walls. Only God can break down what you have built around your heart, a fortress so strong that you have promised yourself never to want to feel hurt like this again. Or perhaps you have given up hope; you have allowed yourself to go adrift in the sea with no direction, no hope of survival, no hope of being found and have sure footing.

Maybe you feel so defeated and broken you are reading this as one last thread of hope. Wherever you are in your journey, please know that God sees you, He knows you, and one day there will be beauty that comes from the ashes of this trial.

Day 1

ISAIAH 61:3 (ESV)

To grant to those who mourn in Zion— to give
them a beautiful headdress instead of ashes,
the oil of gladness instead of mourning, the
garment of praise instead of a faint spirit; that
they may be called oaks of righteousness, the
planting of the LORD, that he may be glorified.

God will be glorified through all the trials, just as it is promised in Isaiah! We will indeed have gladness, praise, joy, and a renewed spirit! These are absolute promises! It may not feel like it now, and perhaps the thought of being happy doesn't even fit; but know that God can heal you, renew you, use your ashes for his Glory! I encourage you to make this your prayer for today; that God will provide what He promised in Isaiah and that you will begin to feel His presence. That gladness will replace mourning, praise will replace sorrow, that you will be seen as an oak of righteousness so that God will be gloried.

Even though you don't feel it now, rest in these promises. Use these as your lighthouse in the storm. Know that you will achieve all that God has for you once the storm passes.

Prayer for today: Dear God, I ask that you cover with me your reassurance and love as I learn to accept that one day I will be healed, that my sorrow will be replaced with praise, my ashes will be used to create only a masterpiece of your design. I pray that you comfort me during this time and give me the peace that passes all understanding. Amen.

Reflections

_____

_____

_____

_____

_____

_____

_____

_____

_____

_____

_____

_____

_____

_____

_____

_____

_____

_____

Day 2

PSALMS 34:18 (NIV)

The Lord is close to the brokenhearted and
saves those who are crushed in spirit

This is one of my favorite verses to just meditate on; that the Lord is close to those who are crushed and broken. That is exactly how we feel when we are grieving; our world has been shattered, broken apart and tossed upside down. But the Lord sees you, He hears you, He knows exactly what you are thinking, feeling, and praying. He is always with us, even when we don't feel Him. This verse reminds us of that. That although our feelings are heavy, there are truths that must not be forgotten or over-shadowed by our feelings. These truths are what the verse says above, so simply, so beautifully.... *"The Lord is close to the brokenhearted, and saves those who are crushed in spirit" Psalms 34:18*

Prayer for today: Dear God, Although I may not feel your presence, you know exactly what I am going through. I ask that you make your presence known to me in a very real and practical way, as I navigate the death of my child.

Only you can provide the peace and reassurance of such a tragedy. Keep me close to you and remind me that you are always nearby. Amen.

Reflections

_____

_____

_____

_____

_____

_____

_____

_____

_____

_____

_____

_____

_____

_____

_____

_____

_____

_____

_____

_____

_____

_____

Day 3

PSALMS 56:8 (NLT)

You keep track of all my sorrows. You have
collected all my tears in your bottle. You have
recorded each one in your book.

Our God has collected our tears and recorded the in-stances of each one of our traumas, our experiences, our heartaches, and our sorrows. I find great comfort in this verse. That God, in His infinite wisdom, presence, and grand duties in Heaven, has taken the time out for me to record my sorrows and catch my tears in a bottle! Can you imagine that!? What an incredibly gentle, compassionate God we serve! He cares enough about us, that He not only comforts us, but He also keeps track of what makes us sad, what has broken our hearts, what we are going through. This verse reminds me that my God is not just some divine being, but a personal, relationship-seeking friend, confi-dant, and father, who cares about all that is happening in my world.

Prayer for today: Dear God, thank you for all that you have promised us. Even though I don't understand why I am going through this storm, I know that you care, that you see me, that you are keeping track of my sorrows. Thank you for caring so deeply about me that you have redeemed me by sending your Son to die for me! As I go through my own child's death, I cannot help but learn better that you also know exactly what it is like to grieve the death of a child! Thank you for caring so deeply for me. Allow me to see this storm through your eyes and learn to rely on you for my strength, healing, and peace. Amen.

Reflections

_____

_____

_____

_____

_____

_____

_____

_____

_____

_____

_____

_____

_____

_____

_____

Day 4

ROMANS 9:2 (NLT)

My Heart is filled with bitter sorrow and un-
ending grief.

Losing a child feels incomprehensible. Our minds and
hearts have a challenging time even acknowledging that
our tragedy is real, and that we won't awake from this
nightmare. This scripture is so poignant and important to
understand our humanness. There are times, like now, that
we are overwhelmed by sadness, sorrow and our grief feel
never-ending. This scripture helps me to understand that
these feelings are God-given, and that I am allowed to feel
grief, sadness, and sorrow. That although God is the ultimate healer, that I am allowed to have a season of grief and
bitterness.

*Prayer for today: Dear God, thank you for allowing
me to have a full range of experiences, emotions, and feelings. Help me to not want to rush through this season of
grief, but lean in and deepen my relationship with you, the
ultimate healer and comforter. Amen.*

Reflections

Day 5

ECCLESIASTES 3: 1-9 (NLT)

[1]For everything there is a season, a time for
every activity under heaven.
[2]A time to be born and a time to die. A time to
plant and a time to harvest.
[3]A time to kill and a time to heal. A time to
tear down and a time to build up.
[4]A time to cry and a time to laugh. A time to
grieve and a time to dance.
[5]A time to scatter stones and a time to gather
stones. A time to embrace and a time to turn
away.
[6]A time to search and a time to quit searching.
A time to keep and a time to throw away.
[7]A time to tear and a time to mend. A time to
be quiet and a time to speak.
[8]A time to love and a time to hate. A time for
war and a time for peace

These passages are a gentle reminder that life has seasons, just as nature has seasons. Seasons are important to help foster growth, renewal, and change. However, none of this is easy, it is often uncomfortable, painful, sometimes unexpected. Much like this grief you are experiencing, nothing can prepare us for what the grief of losing a child feels like. But this scripture can help us remember that the grief will not last forever, that there is a time to grieve, to mourn, to cry, but also to dance, laugh and heal.

Prayer for today: Dear God, help me in this season of grief, mourning, and sadness. Blanket me with your peace, comfort, and healing. Help me through this difficult season and help me become who you want me to be. Amen.

Reflections

_____

_____

_____

_____

_____

_____

_____

_____

_____

_____

_____

_____

Day 6

PSALMS 23:4 (NLT)

Even when I walk through the darkest valley,
I will not be afraid, for you are close beside
me. Your rod and your staff protect and comfort me.

This is truly one of the darkest valleys anyone can walk through. There is little light, lost hope, uncertainty, confusion, anger, despair, sadness, exhaustion. But God promises to be there in the midst of it all. Even when we cannot feel Him, sense Him, see Him, He promises that He is there to comfort us, to be near to us. Don't let your feelings deceive you; God will never leave us or forsake us, even if we cannot feel Him there. There is a great worship song called "Waymaker" by Michael W. Smith, which has these lyrics, *"you never stop, you never stop working, even when I can't see it, you're working, even when I can't feel it, you're working."* God is always with us, even in the darkness, He's working His plan out.

Prayer for today: Dear God, help me remember that even if I cannot feel you, sense you, see you, hear you that

you are always there. You promised to never leave or for-
sake us. I rest in that promise that you are indeed there.
Help me to lean into you and fully rest in your promises,
your comfort, and your guiding hand. Help me not forget
what your word says to hold it fast in my heart, even in my
darkest valleys. Amen.

Reflections

_____

_____

_____

_____

_____

_____

_____

_____

_____

_____

_____

_____

_____

_____

_____

_____

_____

Day 7

HEBREWS 13:5B (NLT)

For God has said, "I will never fail you.
I will never abandon you."

It may not seem like God's in control if He has allowed us to experience the death of our children. In fact, you may be angry at God. You may be fighting feelings of abandonment, bitterness, confusion, anger, despair. God is a big God and can handle hearing what you are feeling, thinking, and experiencing. Perhaps you have refrained from calling out to Him because you are so confused and angry. But I promise that He is a good Father, and He wants you to run to Him. Even though He already knows our hearts, our thoughts, our innermost feelings, He wants you to share that with Him. I encourage you today to cry out to God, be real, be honest, be ugly. Let all of those ugly tears fall. God made you, He knows exactly what you are feeling, experiencing, he knows full well the pain that you are experiencing. We live in a sinful, broken world, but God is always with us, through all the trials and tribulations.

Prayer for today: Dear God, thank you for loving me

through my tears, my pain, and my feelings. This is hard for me to say, but I am angry at you. I do not understand why I am going through this trial; I don't understand why I had to experience the death of my child, but I know you are in control. I know you are a loving, caring God. Help me rest in your comfort and begin to fully express all my emotions and feelings to you, so that you can continue to help me heal. Amen.

Reflections

Day 8

ECCLESIASTES 7:3 (NLT)

Sorrow is better than laughter, for sadness has
a refining influence on us.

At first read this verse doesn't seem hopeful, uplifting, or even helpful. However, just as we have read in the verses this week, there is a season, a time, a reason for our emotions, feelings, and experiences. This verse has a lot of wisdom packed into just a few words; "sadness has a refining influence on us" is such a profound statement. What has sadness, sorrow, grief, and mourning made you realize so far? In my life, it has helped me utterly understand the importance of joy, happiness, and laughter. This may seem like obvious differences to some, but to me, the stark contrast, the vast differences between sorrow and joy are like two ends of completely different spectrums. Until I mourned the loss of my child, I never put much importance or value into feeling good, or happy or even okay. I am not in any way happy that I experienced my losses, but I am glad that God has refined my spirit and soul out of those experiences.

Prayer for today: Dear God, help me see your hand in this journey. Help me allow myself to find the path you have marked for me and allow myself to be refined by you in this process. This journey is not one I would have chosen for myself and often my grief and tears cloud my judgement and sight, however I know you are in control. Help me to rest in your hands, as you refine me through these experiences of sorrow and sadness. Amen.

Reflections

_____

_____

_____

_____

_____

_____

_____

_____

_____

_____

_____

_____

_____

_____

_____

_____

Day 9

ISAIAH 41:10 (NIV)

So do not fear, for I am with you; do not be
dismayed, for I am your God. I will strengthen
you and help you; I will uphold you with my
righteous right hand.

There are 365 verses in the Bible that tell us not to fear: one for each day of the year. I do not think that is some strange coincidence, I genuinely believe that God knew we needed to hear the words "do not fear" every day we are on this earth. I love this verse because it helps show why we don't have to fear. God is with us, He is *our* God, He will supply help, strength, power, and righteousness. How amazing is that? Our powerful creator of the universe will hold us in His right hand. That imagery to me is profound; we are so small, minute, helpless, that we fit in His hand. Yet, He loves us, He sees us in our helpless state, He created us to be wired with our emotions and feelings. He knows full well our needs, desires and wants. He longs to spend time with us and have a close and intimate relationship with Him. How beautiful is that? So, while you walk this journey of grief, know you are not alone. The God of the universe is with you and ready to help you, to strengthen you, to simply hold you.

Prayer for today: Dear God, take away my fears, trepidation, hesitations, and uncertainties. Blanket me with your comfort, love, presence, and peace. Help me fully recognize and understand that even in this dark place, you are with me. Let me never forget your love for me. Amen.

Reflections

_____

_____

_____

_____

_____

_____

_____

_____

_____

_____

_____

_____

_____

_____

_____

_____

Day 10

JEREMIAH 8:18 (NLT)

My grief is beyond healing; my heart is broken

Sometimes, it feels as though we are beyond healing. The simple thought of being happy again almost feels unfair to the child we lost. How can we ever be happy or joyful again when our child has died? How does this make sense? We are shattered. So many writers and authors of the Bible understood grief, especially the grief of losing children. King David understood this personal wound and wrote in Psalms 38:6, "I am bent over and racked with pain. All day long I walk around filled with grief." He knew that grief was not only emotional but physical. Our hearts feel unfixable, we are forever changed. However, there is a hope and peace that is promised to believers. We were never promised a pain-free life, but we were promised peace that passes all understanding. And in this season of grief, I pray that you will begin to experience that peace unlike any other time before.

Prayer for today: Dear God, you know exactly what I am feeling, thinking, experiencing. You have never shield-

ed your children from grief, heartache, or pain, but you promised to be there in the midst of it. I may not understand all that you have planned but help me understand your unfailing love for me. Provide to me the peace that passes all understanding, just as you promised in your scriptures. Allow me to begin to feel this in a new and tangible way. Amen.

Reflections

_____

_____

_____

_____

_____

_____

_____

_____

_____

_____

_____

_____

_____

_____

_____

_____

_____

_____

_____

Day 11

PSALMS 119:50 (NIV)

My comfort in my suffering is this: Your
promise preserves my life.

I am incredibly grateful for this verse; it confirms that God's promises are what keep us moving forward. I also like that it doesn't sugarcoat the experience, the author uses "suffering" and that's exactly what grief is. It is the suffering and subsequent healing of the heart, mind, body, and soul. During this season of grief, we are working on healing in our grief, processing our experiences and allowing the ultimate healer and physician, God, to provide healing from our suffering and pain. As we talked about yesterday, grief can be felt both emotionally and physically, just as King David shared in his writings.

Prayer for today: Dear God, thank you that you promise to comfort us even in our darkest moments. Thank you for meeting us where we are, for allowing us to normalize our experiences of suffering, just as the ancient writers did, but also allow us to rest in your peace, comfort, and healing that we will one day be restored. Amen.

Reflections

Day 12

PROVERBS 16:24 (NIV)

Gracious words are a honeycomb, sweet to the
soul and healing to the bones.

Isn't it true that sweet and gracious words renew our spirit and our mind? Even though we fully understand that words alone cannot simply heal our grief, or change our situation, hearing kindness, mercy, and grace aides in the healing of our heart and mind. In today's verse it says words are a healing to our bones; in this my mind thinks of brokenness, deep pain, unable to move and do what we once did while the healing takes place. Just as a bone heals, so heals our heart in the grieving process. In this same way words can pierce our heart and add more hurts to our wounds. However, I encourage you to not allow the well-meaning words of those around you to take root. As you have already experienced, people don't know what to say and rely on clichés and platitudes which can be well-meaning and intentioned but strike a nerve in us that may bubble up feelings of anger, hurt, and bitterness. If the relationship allows, share with the person who said something hurtful that what they said hurt, but you appreciate their support. If you cannot directly address it, pray that God will remove those words and hurt, and to not allow any damage to occur in your relationships.

Prayer for today: Dear God, help me to not allow any bitterness or hurt from well-meaning friends and family to take root in my heart and mind. Allow me to focus on your words, your sweet promises and those around me who love me and know my journey. Help me to release all that I am holding to you and help me to better hear the healing words. Amen.

Reflections

_____

_____

_____

_____

_____

_____

_____

_____

_____

_____

_____

_____

Day 13

JEREMIAH 17:14 (NIV)

Heal me, Lord, and I will be healed; save me
and I will be saved, for you are the one I
praise.

I love this verse for its simplicity but also the depth of faith it professes. Heal me, save me, and it will be done! As Christians we know the power that God has, but sometimes we can forget, or even over complicate it. Having simple, straightforward faith can allows us to remember that God is in control and that we must allow Him to do His work in our lives. During our grief journey, the Lord will continue to renew you, heal your heart, mind, and spirit, and work out His plan for our lives. Remember that even though we may not understand the trials, grief, and hurt we are experiencing, God loves us and has a plan for us.

Prayer for today: Dear God, allow me to renew my faith in you, and to rid myself of the overcomplications I have adopted. You have promised healing, salvation, wholeness and a plan for our lives and families. Help me to not get caught up in the anxiety, worry, and confusion that has consumed me since the death occurred. Help me to continuously rest in you and look to you for my comfort, healing, and support. Amen.

Reflections

_____

_____

_____

_____

_____

_____

_____

_____

_____

_____

_____

_____

_____

_____

_____

_____

_____

_____

Day 14

ISAIAH 49:13 (NIV)

Shout for joy, you heavens; rejoice, you earth;
burst into song, you mountains! For the Lord
comforts his people and will have compassion
on his afflicted ones.

This verse has so much going on in it! The earth and mountains are singing, rejoicing, but the second half is talking about comfort and compassion for afflicted ones. What do these two things even have in common?! At least that is what I asked myself when I first read this verse. If you read the beginning of this chapter in Isaiah, it is speaking about the greatness and magnitude of God's glorious design, plan, and concern for His creation, including us. Although we are mere creation of God, we are loved, cared for, comforted, healed, supported, protected...etc. If the mountains, heavens, and earth can celebrate God, how much more can we? We can celebrate that we are intimately connected to our creator and although we are going through grief, trials, and tribulations he has not forgotten or forsaken us.

Prayer for today: Dear God, help me remember your ultimate plan for my life, renew my mind and spirit, even in the midst of grief, sorrow, pain and uncertainty. Help me remember that you are still on your throne, you still have a plan, and you are still at work even in the midst of the chaos. Thank you for loving me, having compassion, and providing comfort during this dark time in my life. Amen.

Reflections

_____

_____

_____

_____

_____

_____

_____

_____

_____

_____

_____

_____

_____

_____

_____

_____

_____

_____

Day 15

PSALMS 31:9 (NIV)

Be merciful to me, Lord, for I am in distress;
my eyes grow weak with sorrow, my soul and
body with grief.

As we have learned so far, grief is far more than just an emotional experience, it is a journey that touches our physical, spiritual, mental, and emotional self. Our grief can physically cause pain to our bodies, such as fatigue, lack of appetite, headaches, muscle aches, stomach issues, and other ailments. It can also create hormonal imbalances due to the adrenaline, cortisol, and other natural chemicals in our bodies. Grief can cause cognition issues such as memory loss, inability to focus or concentrate. Grief profoundly affects our entire being, just as this verse shares. Grief is exhausting; however, God is merciful to us and can provide us relief, comfort, and healing in this painful journey.

Prayer for today: Dear God, thank you for providing all my needs, even in this time of grief. Sometimes I don't even know what my needs are, but you are always there to comfort me. Help me to be merciful to myself as I walk through this journey of grief. Continue to provide me with all your mercy, grace, and healing as I continue to navigate these uncharted waters. Amen.

Reflections

_____

_____

_____

_____

_____

_____

_____

_____

_____

_____

_____

_____

_____

_____

_____

_____

_____

_____

_____

Day 16

JOB 17:7 (NIV)

My eyes have grown dim with grief; my whole
frame is but a shadow

Isn't it true that things become distorted while we are grieving? Our perspective is off, our worldview has shifted, and our understating and patience levels usually tank. We have little room for unkindness, platitudes, or even well-meaning words. We are shattered and nothing makes sense; we are often left with more questions than answers. Our brains are clouded, we're tired and nothing is ever the same again. However, there is hope, as we have been reading, God is the provider of comfort and healing. It may not happen as quickly as we would like, but we will be renewed and can feel like we have the energy and wherewithal to start moving forward.

Prayer for today: Dear God, continuously remind me of your presence and plan. Although I am completely shattered, and I have no idea why I am going through this, remain with me. Remind me of your love, sacrifice, and compassion. You understand as a father, you watched your

Son be sacrificed for the entire world, so you know full well the emotional experience of a parent's grief. Even through my darkest days, don't let me forget who holds me in their hands. Amen.

Reflections

_____

_____

_____

_____

_____

_____

_____

_____

_____

_____

_____

_____

_____

_____

_____

_____

_____

_____

_____

_____

Day 17

ISAIAH 40:31 (NIV)

But those who hope in the Lord will renew their strength. They will soar on wings
like eagles; they will run and not grow weary;
they will walk and not be faint.

This is truly one of my favorite verses. There is so much hope and promise! I love how the verse uses the word *will*, as in it is happening! We will soar in wings of eagles, we will run and not grow weary, we will walk and not be faint all because we have hope and faith in the Lord and He has provided a renewed strength within us. What an amazing promise to focus on, especially in this time of grief.

Prayer for today: Dear God, thank you for your promises of strength, renewal, and hope. Although my life is different now, I know you will provide all that I need to continue to move forward and heal. And although my heart will always miss my child, and I will always carry some of the grief with me, you will heal me in a way that I can continue to live a life that is a testimony to you. Amen.

Reflections

Day 18

1 PETER 5:10 (NIV)

And the God of all grace, who called you
to his eternal glory in Christ, after you have
suffered a little while, will himself restore you
and make you strong, firm, and steadfast.

All throughout the scriptures there are promises of grace, renewal, and restoration! Although you may feel broken, unusable, forever changed, God has a plan for your life, your brokenness, your testimony and for your restoration. Even though you may be shattered now, you will be made whole, restored to a beautiful new creation. This renewal reminds me of the Japanese custom of fixing broken pots with gold with the idea of instead of hiding the brokenness it becomes a part of the pot's history, journey, story. Isn't that just like God? He uses our brokenness, our scars, our hurts to highlight His plan, and His ability to create something even more unique and beautiful than the original!

Prayer for today: Dear God, thank you that even though I am currently broken you are fixing me with gold!

Your vision for my life is beyond my comprehension, but I know that once you are done healing me, mending my broken parts, and putting me back together I will be even more beautiful than my original self! Amen.

Reflections

_____

_____

_____

_____

_____

_____

_____

_____

_____

_____

_____

_____

_____

_____

_____

_____

_____

_____

_____

_____

_____

Day 19

JEREMIAH 18:6 (NIV)

He said, "Can I not do with you, Israel, as
this potter does?" declares the Lord. "Like
clay in the hand of the potter, so are you in
my hand, Israel."

I love the analogy of God as the potter, and we are the clay. We often feel disjointed, unsettled, not right, and broken but God is continuously molding, shaping, and working on us to make us into the beautiful creation He has designed. He sees the finish product as He is working on us, and as He smooths out our rough edges, or fixes our broken pieces, He knows that in the end we will glorify Him with our beauty and purpose.

Prayer for today: Dear God, I know you have designed me for a purpose, even if I don't fully understand what it is. I also understand that going through this grief will allow you to continue to teach, shape and mold me into who you have called me to be. I may not understand your reasons, purposes or even understand what I will be like in the end, but I am trusting you as the Potter and I submit to you as clay. Amen.

Reflections

_____

_____

_____

_____

_____

_____

_____

_____

_____

_____

_____

_____

_____

_____

_____

_____

_____

_____

_____

_____

_____

_____

_____

_____

Day 20

PSALMS 91:2 (NIV)

I will say of the Lord, "He is my refuge and
my fortress, my God, in whom I trust.

Trusting God through our storms is a lot easier said than done. It is easier to sit back and declare that yes, of course, I will praise God through every trial and tribulation, just as Paul shared in his writings. However, when we are in the midst of the storm we often flail, waver, and become disoriented. This verse is often used in conjunction with the picture of a lighthouse with waves crashing against it. I love this image because when we are grieving the loss of our children, the waves of grief are large, unwavering, relentless, strong, fierce, and powerful; however, God is our lighthouse. We are not the lighthouse; we are kept inside the lighthouse. If God is our fortress, then that means He is what is keeping us from the crashing waves. We might feel the residual, feal the fear, have no idea when the storm is ending, but God remains strong, steadfast, trustworthy, upright.

Prayer for today: Dear God, thank you for being my strong fortress, my rock, my salvation. You keep me pro-

tected even though I am fearful, uncertain, or disoriented,
you remain with me and cover me in your love, compas-
sion and understanding. Amen.

Reflections

_____
_____
_____
_____
_____
_____
_____
_____
_____
_____
_____
_____
_____
_____
_____
_____
_____
_____
_____
_____
_____

Day 21

JOSHUA 1:9 (NIV)

Be strong and courageous. Do not be afraid;
do not be discouraged, for the Lord your God
will be with you wherever you go."

This verse is very direct in its instructions; we are NOT to be afraid or discouraged and we ARE to be strong and courageous because the Lord is with us wherever we go. Even in the trenches of our grief, in our darkest storms, in our lowest moods, God sees us, He knows us. Nothing is hidden from Him. There is so much hope in that. Even though we must intentionally choose courage and strength over fear and discouragement, God is still with us. Even when it feels as though He has abandoned us, or as though He has stolen our precious child. These are not true. The scriptures remind us that He only has good for us, however, He does allow things to happen in our lives. And sometimes awful things happen simply because we live in a broken, sinful world and the devil is creating non-stop chaos. But our hope is in the Lord! We know that we have a hope and a future, even when we don't feel like it.

Prayer for today: Dear God, even when I don't feel you, you are there. Even when I am discouraged, you are there. No matter what I am feeling, experiencing, or going through, you are still there. Help to remember that my feelings are helpful tools, but they are not always the truth. Remind me that you are there, you've never left, and you are still working in the background. Amen.

Reflections

_____

_____

_____

_____

_____

_____

_____

_____

_____

_____

_____

_____

_____

_____

_____

_____

_____

_____

Day 22

ISAIAH 45:18 (NLT)

For the Lord is God, and he created the heavens and earth and put everything in place. He made the world to be lived in, not to be a place of empty chaos. "I am the Lord," he says, "and there is no other.

I love that this verse is so direct and reaffirms that God is not a God of chaos, but of order; everything has a place. Although your world may seem chaotic, unhinged out of order, confusing, overwhelming, God still is in control. We live in a broken, sinful, chaotic world, but not because God created it that way; man's actions and decisions and sinful desires created the chaos. So, take heart, that although everything is out of place, in disarray, upside down, God is still on His throne. He still has a plan, and everything will be made right one day.

Prayer for today: Dear God, even though I know in my mind that you are in control my heart is speaking other things. Help me to take all my thoughts captive and meditate on today's verse, that you are indeed THE LORD, there is no other and you are not a god of chaos! You cre-

ated order, and one day order will indeed be restored, and my heart, mind, and body will be healed, and I will get to see my child again! Amen.

Reflections

_____

_____

_____

_____

_____

_____

_____

_____

_____

_____

_____

_____

_____

_____

_____

_____

_____

_____

_____

_____

Day 23

2 CORINTHIANS 10:5 (NIV)

We demolish arguments and every pretension
that sets itself up against the knowledge of
God, and we take captive every thought to
make it obedient to Christ.

The wilderness of grief, as Dr. Alan Wolfelt calls it, is a bleak, uncharted, desolate place. It is lonely, confusing, and often contradictory to our faith. We have so many questions, so many thoughts, so many emotions. This verse is a one that I often recite to myself as I know that my feelings and emotions can be deceitful and that feelings are not facts. So often I must reconcile my thoughts against the truths, promises and record of God's word. If my thoughts, feelings, or emotions contradicts what I know to be true about God or His plan, then I need to "take them captive" as the verse says.

Prayer for today: Dear God, help me to take all my thoughts captive and stay grounded in your word, your promises, and your truth. Help me to make this a daily practice as I navigate this journey of grief. Amen.

Reflections

Day 24

PSALMS 146:5 (NLT)

But joyful are those who have the God of
Israel as their helper, whose hope is in the
LORD their God.

Happiness and joy can seem so foreign these days, so out of touch, so wrong, and perhaps the thought of being happy again brings pings of pain and guilt. Being joyful after all this hurt doesn't even seem possible or even fair. I have had grieving mothers share with me that the thought of living happy lives doesn't seem right or even possible after the heartache they have been through. But God....

God promises us His joy, His happiness, His goodness. Although it may seem foreign now, if we rest in Him and keep steadfast in our faith, we will again experience a renewal of mind, body, and spirit.

Prayer for today: Dear God, although my heart cannot even begin to fathom joy and happiness right now, I know these are promises from you. As I continue to move through this grief, continue to remind me of your promises and surround me with all that I am lacking as you are the only one that can. Amen.

Reflections

Day 25

JEREMIAH 29:11 (NLT)

For I know the plans I have for you," says the Lord. "They are plans for good and not for disaster, to give you a future and a hope.

Everyone who has been a Christian for even a minute has seen, heard, read, or had this verse quoted to them. Some families I have counseled relay that this verse is overused, and they often feel as though if this verse were true, then they wouldn't be experiencing the grief and heartache they are. However, I see this verse differently; it is not a verse for now, but for our future. As we have talked about earlier this week, we live in a broken world. And although God is not orchestrating the chaos, Satan is. God does indeed have plans for a good hopeful future. He wouldn't have sent His Son, Jesus, if this weren't true. God has had a plan for our redemption the moment Adam and Eve sinned.

Prayer for today: Dear God, remind me often of your perfect and redemptive plan for my life. Although I am ex-

periencing pain, grief, anguish, and heartache you have made a way for my healing. You alone can mend the whole that has been left in my heart by the death of my child. You alone know the depths of sorrow. Thank you for always being there, a daily companion even when I don't feel you. Amen.

Reflections

_____

_____

_____

_____

_____

_____

_____

_____

_____

_____

_____

_____

_____

_____

_____

_____

_____

_____

Day 26

HEBREWS 6:19 (NLT)

This hope is a strong and trustworthy anchor
for our souls. It leads us through the curtain
into God's inner sanctuary.

I have lived in Maryland my entire life, and if you know anything about Maryland geography we are surrounded by water, more specifically the Chesapeake Bay. Marylanders are a proud people that celebrate all things related to the bay, including the famous blue crabs, sailing, and all things nautical. So, the visual of anchors and curtains within this verse are familiar to me; however, this may not be the case for you. Nevertheless, I want you to take a moment and visualize an anchor. What does it look like? What is its purpose? What is it made of?

I genuinely believe that God has provided the visual of an anchor in this verse because of what the anchor is responsible for. Anchors are significantly smaller than the vessels they're responsible for, but are strong, powerful, and trustworthy. That is what God is promising in this verse; although something like hope seems small, it has power and promise!

Prayer for today: Dear God, although some days seem hopeless, please don't let me lose sight of your hope. You promised in this verse that Hope is a trustworthy and strong anchor for our souls. Help me to always remember that even though I go through rough storms, trials, and tribulations, your hope holds me steadfast. Amen.

Reflections

_____

_____

_____

_____

_____

_____

_____

_____

_____

_____

_____

_____

_____

_____

_____

_____

_____

_____

Day 27

PSALMS 62:5 (NLT)

Let all that I am wait quietly before God, for
my hope is in him.

Hope has been our theme these last few days. This is
not by coincidence, but a strategic compass through the
grief journey. If we do not have hope as our anchor, as the
verse yesterday stated, we are tossed at sea, no plan, no direction, no end in sight. Hope is not something that we can
maintain on our own; hope requires intentionality. This
simply means we do not just happen upon hope, we do not
just feel it out of nowhere. We must *find* hope. The verse
for today talks about waiting quietly before God because
our hope *is in Him.* Did you catch that? Our hope is only
found IN Him. Which means that we must intentionally,
faithfully, and often quietly rely on God because He is the
source of our hope, He is our anchor, but more importantly,
He is our compass.

*Prayer for today: Dear God, sometimes I forget that
you are sovereign, almighty, above all and in control of*

all. And even though you have allowed Satan the ability to roam the earth and orchestrate chaos, nothing can be done without your knowledge or approval. You are the ultimate guide, compass, and helper. There is nothing in this world that I need that you cannot provide. Help me to lean more into your love, your guidance, and provisions; help me learn to better allow you to lead instead of me. Forgive me for my forgetfulness of your love, hope, ability, sovereignty, and holiness. Amen.

Reflections

_____

_____

_____

_____

_____

_____

_____

_____

_____

_____

_____

_____

_____

Day 28

GALATIANS 5:16 (NLT)

So, I say, let the Holy Spirit guide your lives.
Then you won't be doing what your sinful
nature craves.

God's plan for our lives is wonderfully mysterious, intricate, and thoughtfully planned out. He has provided the Holy Spirit as our practical compass, He is the one who pulls our hearts in the correct direction, prompts our thoughts, reminds us to recenter ourselves in God's will and plan. Now you may be wondering why the death of your child was in God's plan, or how could that be part of the wonderfully thought-out idea of a loving God. But remember, God is not creating the chaos, Satan is, therefore although God is not wanting us to experience death, heartache, and grief, He is able to use the awful plans of Satan and this sinful world to remind us that we are in desperate need of God and His plans. Humanity alone is lost, cursed, and broken and in serious need for rescuing…cue Jesus.

God knew all along that man was imperfect, so He created an exit strategy that Satan cannot defeat, no matter what tactics he employs. Jesus is our only hope.

Prayer for today: Dear God, I have no idea why the death of my child was allowed in your plan, or what purpose this experience will serve in your divine will. But no matter what I will trust in you, I will not lose sight of your ultimate plan to redeem humanity through the death of your Son, Jesus. You understand what it feels like for a parent to experience the death of their child. Continue to remind me gently of your Holy Spirit's intentions and will in my life as my compass, and helper; and to avoid my sinful nature's desires. Amen.

Reflections

_____

_____

_____

_____

_____

_____

_____

_____

_____

_____

_____

_____

Day 29

PSALMS 43:3 (NLT)

Send out your light and your truth; let them
guide me. Let them lead me to your holy
mountain, to the place where you live.

Anchors, lights, beacons, lamps; all symbols used in the Bible to help us visualize and understand God's desire, plan, and purpose for us. God is love, light, and truth; everything else is false, dark, deceitful. If we rest in His truth, allow the Holy Spirit to speak truth and light into our minds, hearts, and lives, we will be restored and healed. The thought of healing and restoration may seem like a distant, unrealistic dream, but you will be whole again. But being whole doesn't mean back to who you were before the death of your child. You will forever be changed and different, but that doesn't mean un-healthy, or unhealed. This journey may be a long one for you, as timelines don't really exist in uncharted territory. But don't lose sight of God's love and desire for you.

Prayer for today: Dear God, even though I am in the wilderness of my grief, I can rest in the truth that there is an end to my pain, grief, and sorrow. You have provided a way to healing, wholeness and redemption. Amen.

Reflections

_____
_____
_____
_____
_____
_____
_____
_____
_____
_____
_____
_____
_____
_____
_____
_____
_____
_____
_____
_____
_____
_____
_____
_____
_____
_____
_____
_____
_____

Day 30

PSALMS 48:14 (NLT)

For that is what God is like. He is our God
forever and ever, and he will guide us
until we die.

No matter what we are going through, no matter our doubts, fears, anger, emotions, confusion, heartbreak, uncertainty, bad decisions…God is there. Just as the Psalmist said, He is our God forever and ever. As long we stay connected to our faith and allow the Holy Spirit to guide us and comfort us, we will always have what we need. Through this journey of grief, God will continue to lead us through. Even King David wrote about God's provision through darkness, uncertainty, and grief. We may not have all the answers, and we may not fully understand this journey we are on, but we have a God who loves us; and will never leave nor forsake us.

Prayer for today: Dear God, as I continue to make my way through my grief journey, I pray that you will put people in my path to help me. Allow those vetted by the Holy Spirit to come along side me and help me in my healing.

You have created us to be with others, and it is not healthy to always isolate. I pray your guidance, wisdom, and direction for the next steps of this journey. Amen.

Reflections

_____

_____

_____

_____

_____

_____

_____

_____

_____

_____

_____

_____

_____

_____

_____

_____

_____

_____

_____

_____

Day 31

ROMANS 15:13 (NLT)

I pray that God, the source of hope, will fill
you completely with joy and peace because
you trust in him. Then you will overflow with
confident hope through the power of the Holy
Spirit.

Today's verse is truly my prayer for you; that God will completely overwhelm you with His peace, love, and comfort. So much so that you have no doubts that He is alive and working within your life.

We may never know, understand, or fully comprehend why we had to experience the death of our children, but we do know we believe in a God who is working for our good, even in a world filled with chaos.

Prayer for today: Dear God, my grief journey is not over, and I have so many more questions; however, I know for certain that you love me, care for me and know who I am and what is going on in my heart, life, and family. I pray for your healing in all aspects of my body, life, heart, mind, and family as we all grieve together, but in our unique ways. Thank you for all your promises! Amen.

Reflections

Epilogue

Even though this devotional was only thirty-one days long, I pray it has brought some comfort and hope to your life. Your grief journey is not over yet, but I pray you allow God to break down the walls you have built, to soften the rough edges this death has caused and that you begin to truly experience love, forgiveness, healing, and redemption unlike any time before.

The death of a child never makes sense, and truly only God knows why we must experience such pain. But my faith and trust are greater than my hurt, doubt, or uncertainty. If I don't retain my hope in Christ, than I am nothing more than a ship without an anchor.

It has only been one year since my last miscarriage, but I can speak truthfully that even through the pain of losing so many pregnancies, I truly believe that there is reason God allowed me to walk through those trials. I may not know the reason on this side of heaven, but I trust in His divine will and plan. Just as Jesus trusted that His death on a cross was what was needed and intended for humanity, I trust that God has allowed me to walk through heartache for a reason only known to Him at this moment.

I encourage you to seek people out that have experienced similar journeys but have also experienced healing and reconciliation. Look for grief support groups specifically for grieving parents, join a small group at your church, continue to force yourself out of isolation and distraction and be intentional about healing your grief.

As you walk through this grief journey, do not assign yourself a timeline, as everyone's grief journey and healing occur at different times. Try to refrain from comparing your grief to anyone else's, this comparison game can create additional feelings of anger, bitterness, and confusion. Trust in God, remain steadfast in your faith, and allow God to wrap you in His peace, comfort, and presence.

My prayer for you is that through this difficult journey of grief, pain and hurt, God will reveal Himself to you unlike any time before. That you will completely surrender to His will, and allow Him to heal, renew and create something beautiful out of your story and experiences.

Printed in the USA
CPSIA information can be obtained
at www.ICGtesting.com
LVHW021608121023
760666LV00017B/1198